MOON
LANDING

Essential Events

MOON
LANDING

BY NADIA HIGGINS

Content Consultant
James Flaten, Ph.D.
Associate Director, Minnesota Space Grant Consortium
University of Minnesota, Minneapolis, Minnesota

ABDO
Publishing Company

CREDITS

Published by ABDO Publishing Company, 8000 West 78th Street, Edina, Minnesota
55439. Copyright © 2008 by Abdo Consulting Group, Inc. International
copyrights reserved in all countries. No part of this book may be reproduced in
any form without written permission from the publisher. The Essential
Library™is a trademark and logo of ABDO Publishing Company.

Printed in the United States.

Editor: Patricia Stockland
Cover Design: Becky Daum
Interior Design: Lindaanne Donohoe

Library of Congress Cataloging-in-Publication Data
Higgins, Nadia.
  Moon landing / Nadia Higgins.
    p. cm. — (Essential events)
  Includes bibliographical references and index.
  ISBN-13: 978-1-59928-854-3
  1. Project Apollo (U.S.)—Juvenile literature. 2. Space flight to the moon—
Juvenile literature. 3. Apollo 11 (Spacecraft)—Juvenile literature. I. Title.
TL789.8.U6A535254 2008
  629.45'4—dc22   2007012152

TABLE OF CONTENTS

Neil Armstrong, Michael Collins, and Edwin "Buzz" Aldrin, the Apollo 11 *crew*

LIFT OFF

The three astronauts lay on their backs in the command module of the *Apollo 11* spacecraft, their boots locked in titanium clamps above their heads. Their upper bodies were strapped tight against the couches. Inside their bulky space suits, they could barely even lift their arms—though now it did not matter much.

Inside a capsule the size of a walk-in closet, the men were perched on top of the most powerful rocket in the world. As tall as a 36-story building, the *Saturn V* rocket packed as much power as a small nuclear weapon.

For months, the men had endured exhausting training. For almost a decade, 400,000 people had worked toward it. Neil Armstrong, Edwin "Buzz" Aldrin, and Michael Collins were about to blast off to the moon. The day, July 16, 1969, marked the beginning of what former President John Kennedy had called "the most hazardous and dangerous and greatest adventure on which man has ever embarked."[1]

The men had awakened at 4:15 that morning in the dormitory rooms of the Manned Spacecraft Operations Building near Cape Canaveral, Florida. After a brief medical exam, they ate their quick breakfast of steak, eggs, toast, coffee, and juice.

At 5:30 a.m., they began the hour-long process of suiting up. With the help of "suit techs," they

Moving Target

The moon is constantly moving through space, making a full orbit around Earth every 27.3 days. The journey to the moon from Earth was going to take 66 hours. So the *Apollo 11* spacecraft was aimed not at the moon, but at where the moon would be in three days.

struggled into their stiff, white pressure suits. The suits were an essential safety precaution. If anything went wrong during liftoff, the suit was like its own mini-spacecraft, protecting the astronaut against the extreme hazards of outer space. Next, a fishbowl-like bubble helmet was screwed into a metal ring on the suit's collar. Now the men could only communicate through the radio headsets in their helmets.

After suiting up, Armstrong, Aldrin, and Collins made their way to the transfer van that would carry them to Launch Complex 39's Pad A. They walked down a corridor where their friends and family had gathered to see them off. Through their soundproof helmets, the men watched the silent commotion. They hugged their families and waved their final, wordless goodbyes.

At 6:52 a.m., they arrived at the launch pad. They took a 32-second elevator ride to the top of the launch tower, a red structure attached to the rocket by several long, metal arms.

The astronauts met the "close out" team for one last inspection in the tent-like "white room" by the hatch of the command module. Then it was time to board. They squeezed into their positions inside the spacecraft. The hatch was sealed. The last technicians

Apollo 11 crew members, led by Neil Armstrong, make their way to the transfer van, in preparation for launch.

cleared the area. Now the astronauts were the only people within three miles (5 km) of the launch pad. At the Launch Control Center, panel lights blinked on— green for go.

So much was at stake. Just two-and-a-half years earlier, three astronauts had died during a trial run of this very mission. The rocket depended on the perfect working order of millions of parts—and often with split-second timing. Technicians had run through a checklist 30,000 pages long in preparation for this flight.

"The launch is the time when you are more conscious than any other time of your dependence on machinery," Collins later wrote. "You worry mightily that the rocket is going to veer off course or stop or explode …"[2] Were the astronauts safe?

The time was 9:27 a.m.—five minutes

The *Saturn V*

The *Saturn V* weighed 6.5 million pounds (2.9 million kg), almost all of which was liquid oxygen fuel. The hull of the rocket was remarkably light and thin. The rocket's metal casing was never more than ¼-inch (6 mm) thick and in other places thinner than household aluminum foil. It would have been too heavy to get off the ground otherwise.

Saturn V stood 363 feet (111 m) high and was 33 feet (10 m) across at its widest point. If the pencil-shaped rocket were laid on its side, it would have been longer than a football field.

Simply housing and moving such an enormous rocket required separate engineering feats. A special, 52-story Vehicle Assembly Building (VAB) was built on Cape Canaveral in order to assemble the *Saturn V*. By volume, the VAB was the largest building in the world.

To move the rocket from the VAB to the launch pad, another record-breaker was created. The crawler-transporter, a two-story moving platform, was the largest land vehicle ever made. As it carried the rocket along the gravel road to the launch pad, it crushed the stones beneath it.

until liftoff. Below, at a viewing grandstand, along the beaches and in stopped cars on the highway, one million people had gathered to watch the rocket launch. Millions more watched around the world on television. Some of the people gathered at the Cape had come to protest the launch. Today, most Americans look back at the first moon landing as one of their country's proudest moments. In 1969, however, when social problems and the Vietnam War troubled the nation, many wondered if the billions of dollars spent on going to the moon would be better spent elsewhere. Would they be proven right?

Packing for the Trip

Each astronaut was allowed to bring only eight ounces (228 g) worth of personal items onboard. The men packed their PPKs, or personal preference kits, with small items of sentimental value such as good-luck charms, army medals, and family photos.

And, most importantly, what about the Soviets? The Soviet Union (now Russia) was the United States' most feared enemy. The two nations were engaged in the Cold War. Instead of waging real war, each tried to intimidate the other through shows of superior military and technological power. In 1957, the Soviets had stunned the world by sending the first satellites to outer space. Since then, the United States had been trying to

Pressure Suits

The suits that the astronauts wore during liftoff each cost about $100,000. Each was made up of more than 500 separate parts and weighed between 35 and 50 pounds (16 and 23 kg). The astronauts called the suits "moon cocoons." Inside was everything they needed to survive in space. The suit's pressure kept an astronaut's lungs from popping in the vacuum of space. It regulated extreme heat and cold, and it provided water, oxygen, and protection from deadly pieces of flying dust, called micrometeoroids.

catch up in what came to be called the "space race."

Achieving more "firsts" in space was a constant spur behind the entire moon program. What could be a better show of power than landing an expedition on the moon? At the same time, what could be more disastrous than trying and failing in front of the whole world? In 1969, the U.S. National Aeronautics and Space Administration (NASA) was still a new program. Could the young NASA survive such a public-relations fiasco?

The astronauts themselves could not afford to contemplate such worries. They appeared confident, though, as Armstrong would later remark,

We were certainly not overconfident. In … exploration, the unexpected is always expected. … On the morning of July 16, 1969, we knew that hundreds of thousands of Americans had given their best effort to give us this chance. Now it was time for us to give our best.[3]

The countdown rang out at the grandstand and inside the helmets of the men.

T minus twelve … eleven … ten

At "T minus nine"—nine seconds left—fireballs shot out of the engines and into the fire trench below. An enormous gush of water flooded the fire, creating billowing white clouds of smoke as temperatures reached 1,900 degrees Fahrenheit (1,000° C). Shards of ice cascaded off the rocket—frozen condensation vibrating off the supercooled tanks of liquid oxygen fuel. Everyone within 10 miles (16 km) felt the rocket rumble. At the grandstand, viewers gasped for breath as the sonic roar shook their lungs and grabbed their stomachs.

Aboard *Apollo 11*, the men heard only a distant roar through their helmets. But they felt the force of the rocket shake them so hard, they could no longer see clearly. The buttons and lights on the control panel were all a blur.

Ominous Bulge

Would the moon mission be foiled by something as small as a bulging pouch on the left leg of Neil Armstrong's pressure suit? As the men lay strapped into their couches, they worried that the pouch lay awfully close to the spaceship's abort handle. During take-off, the spacecraft would be violently shaken. What if Armstrong's pocket accidentally snagged on the handle?

Six ... five ... four ...

The rocket had come to life—a spitting, shaking, fire-breathing beast, ready to rip into the sky. But the creature needed 7.7 million pounds (3.5 million kg) of thrust, or force, to power it into space against the pull of Earth's gravity. As the rocket approached full thrust, four arms from the red launch tower pinned it to the ground.

Three ... two ... one ... zero.

Explosives fired and released the arms.

Liftoff!

Then the rocket rose, at first just slightly above the launch pad. For a full ten seconds, it slowly climbed the height of the launch tower. Just seconds later, though, the rocket was flying at a rate of 6 miles (10 km) per second. The rocket shot through the sky, a stream of fire trailing behind it. The 240,000-mile (386,000-km) journey to the moon was off to a flawless start.

Clouds of smoke billow around Saturn V during liftoff.

Early experiments with rockets would inspire later efforts toward space travel.

THE RACE TO THE MOON

*T*he idea behind any rocket is that it can power a ship through the vacuum of space. It does not require air or any other source of friction to push against. As the rocket burns fuel, it creates a powerful stream of exhaust. The exhaust comes out the rear of the rocket. Scientists know that this force pushes the rocket forward. They relied on the classic law of physics, developed in the late 1600s by Isaac Newton: For every action, there is an equal and opposite reaction.

In the early 1900s, scientists began to experiment with rockets in their private laboratories and backyards. In 1926, the American scientist Robert Goddard launched the first rocket using liquid fuel, a key feature of later space rockets. Goddard's early rockets rose just over 200 feet (61 m) into the air, but they inspired further efforts. Around the world, scientists published articles and discussed their work at meetings.

In World War II, Germany's Nazi leader Adolph Hitler took a sudden interest in rockets—but not for space exploration. Hitler developed a state-of-the-art research center to develop rockets for launching deadly missiles.

Moon Myths

Some early myths about the moon are still familiar today. Stories of werewolves howling at the full moon and vampires coming to life by the moon's glow were started by Europeans in the Middle Ages. They also observed that a full moon has dark spots that make it look like a person's face, giving rise to stories of the "Man in the Moon." Medieval Europeans were less sure about what the moon was actually made of. A popular folktale insisted it was green cheese. Others believed the moon was a wafer-thin disk, made of a perfectly smooth substance.

Moon Milestones

The ancient Greek astronomer Hipparchus first calculated the moon's size and distance from Earth in 130 B.C. Italian astronomer Galileo Galilei was the first to view the moon through a telescope in 1609. He was amazed to see that the perfect circle in the sky was covered with mountains and craters. In 1651, Giovanni Battista Riccoli labeled these features in the moon's first map with poetic, otherworldly names such as the Sea of Tranquility, the Bay of Rainbows, and the Lake of Dreams. Armstrong and Aldrin's historic moon walk was on the Sea of Tranquility, which proved not to be a sea at all, but a large, flat plain.

After Germany's defeat, that technology was delivered into U.S. hands by one of Hitler's own scientists, Wernher von Braun. Germany's research brought the idea of moon travel into the realm of possibility.

By the 1960s, the ancient interest in the moon was as strong as ever. Advances in rocket science had made moon travel at least plausible. What was needed now was the will to do it. After all, such a project was no small undertaking. It would cost billions of dollars and take the work of thousands of people.

The threat of war took the dream of space travel and made it real. During the 1960s, the Cold War was at its height. The United States and the Soviet Union competed to show which was the stronger superpower. The United States wanted a world of independent, democratically elected governments where private businesses could flourish. The Soviet Union advocated communism, a system in which government controlled almost every aspect of people's lives.

"Any idea that the Apollo program [to reach the moon] was a great voyage of exploration or scientific endeavor is nuts," said Frank Borman, an astronaut on the 1968 mission around the moon. "People just aren't that excited about exploration. They were sure excited about beating the Russians."[1]

Outer space became the arena for the "space race," a powerful competition between the United States and the Soviet Union. While the race was symbolic, the consequences were real. In the eyes of the Americans, winning the space race meant winning the Cold War. They hoped it would stop the spread of communism. "Beating the Russians" in space was also the best way to scare the enemy—and keep real war at bay.

Americans knew firsthand the terror of losing the symbolic contest. On October 4, 1957, the Soviet Union sent the first satellite into Earth's orbit. For about three months, *Sputnik I* circled Earth every 96 minutes. As the 184-pound (83-kg) ball hurtled along, it sent out a beeping radio signal that the Soviets proudly broadcast around the world.

Americans were shocked. The Soviets had reached outer space first. Did that mean that they had the ability to launch a nuclear warhead? Were they planning an attack from outer space? Rumors spread wildly.

The nation was still reeling when *Sputnik II* blasted into space almost one month later. This satellite was 1,100 pounds (499 kg), and it carried a crew member—a dog named Laika. *Sputnik II* soon became Laika's coffin, however, as the dog died from stress and overheating shortly after launch. The satellite orbited for 162 days with Laika's body inside it.

The United States tried desperately to catch up with the Soviets. In December, the Navy tried to launch its

Werner von Braun, Rocket Scientist

As the Nazi government rose to power and war loomed in his country, a young German engineering student followed a dream. He studied and built rockets, hoping that one day his work would lead to great adventures in outer space. After World War II broke out, however, Germany's Nazi government eyed von Braun's passion with another purpose. Rockets could also shoot deadly missiles at Germany's enemies.

Werner von Braun was faced with a difficult choice: he could develop rockets for the military, or he could quit his profession altogether. Von Braun accepted the offer, secretly hoping that the war would end before his rocket was developed.

Von Braun's wish did not come true. The rockets that he and a team of 10,000 engineers developed became the Nazi's Vengeance Weapon, the V-2.

As the war continued and the Nazis faced surrender, they ordered von Braun's research destroyed in order to keep it from falling into enemy hands. Von Braun came up with a plan to save his work. Along with a group of 500 fellow scientists, he smuggled the materials south.

By 1960, von Braun was developing space rockets for NASA. Though begun in wartime Germany, his precious research led directly to the *Saturn V* rocket that launched the first American astronauts to the moon.

own satellite, but the rocket exploded one inch off the launch pad.

Finally, on January 31, 1958, almost four months after *Sputnik I*, the United States moved forward in the space race with the successful launch of *Explorer I*. However, the tiny satellite weighed a disappointing 18.13 pounds (8.23 kg). In May, the Soviets clearly jumped ahead with the launch of the 2,900-pound (1,300-kg) *Sputnik III*. Soviet leader Nikita Khrushchev referred to the U.S. satellites as "oranges."

In July 1958, President Dwight D. Eisenhower signed a bill creating NASA. The space race was fully on. By the fall, NASA announced Project Mercury. The project's goal was to send an American into space. NASA looked to military test pilots to serve as the nation's first astronauts, and hundreds of pilots volunteered for the project. From these, NASA chose seven who became instant heroes. Known as the Mercury Seven, the men represented their nation's deepest hopes and fears.

While America's first astronauts trained, the Soviets surprised the world with another space success. In the fall of 1959, they sent two unmanned probes to the moon. The space race became one of the nation's top issues during the 1960 presidential campaign.

Sturdy Stuff

The Mercury Seven astronauts were chosen from a pool of 508 applicants. Before being hired, they under went vigorous tests and interviews. In one series of tests, they were subjected to extreme heat, noise, and vibrations to see how well they would stand up to the stress of flying in outer space. It is no wonder author Tom Wolfe picked *The Right Stuff* as the title for his book about these men. Wolfe's book was later adapted into a movie by the same name.

A young Democratic candidate from Massachusetts, John F. Kennedy, inspired the country with his vision for the future. Once in office, President Kennedy consulted his advisors. What space project could clearly put the United States ahead in the space race?

Then, on April 12, 1961, the stakes were dramatically raised when the Soviets sent a man into space. Yuri Gagarin flew 108 minutes, completing one full Earth orbit aboard *Vostok 1*.

"Let the other capitalist countries catch up with our country, which has blasted the trail into outer space," boasted Khrushchev.[2]

In an April 20 memo to Vice President Lyndon Johnson, Chairman of the Space Council, President Kennedy wrote,

> *Do we have a chance of beating the Soviets by putting a laboratory in space, or by a trip around the moon, or by a rocket to land on the moon ... Is there any other space program which promises dramatic results in which we could*

win? … Are we working 24 hours a day on existing programs? If not, why not?[3]

Johnson wrote back that landing an expedition on the moon was the only answer:

> *In the eyes of the world, first in space is first, period. Second in space is second in everything.[4]*

Was a trip to the moon feasible? The United States was struggling with serious social issues such as poverty and racism. How could Kennedy convince the public to undertake such a massive, expensive mission?

Kennedy got his answer on May 5, 1961, the day Alan Shepard Jr. became the first American to go into space. Compared to Gagarin's, Shepard's flight was not impressive. He flew for just 15 minutes in an arch peaking at 117 miles (188 km). Nevertheless, the American public reacted with overwhelming pride.

A Tall Order

On September 12, 1962, President Kennedy delivered another speech about going to the moon. This time, he provided specifics: "We shall send to the moon, more than 240,000 miles from the control station in Houston, a giant rocket more than 300 feet tall, ... made of new metal alloys, some of which have not yet been invented, capable of standing heat and stresses several times more than have ever been experienced, fitted together with a precision better than the finest watch, carrying all the equipment needed for propulsion, guidance, control, communications, food and survival, on an untried mission to an unknown celestial body. ..."[5]

Kennedy now knew what had to be done. He addressed Congress on May 25, 1961 with strong words:

> ... the dramatic achievements in space which occurred in recent weeks should have made clear to us all ... the impact of this adventure on the minds of men everywhere ...
>
> I believe this nation should commit itself to achieving the goal, before this decade is out, of landing a man on the moon and returning him safely to Earth.[6]

At NASA, people were shocked. They had yet to even send an astronaut into Earth's orbit. Here was the president talking about going to the moon—and with a deadline. Nevertheless, the path to the moon had begun.

Almost nine months later, on February 20, 1962, the United States made a major advance in the space race. On that day, John Glenn became the first American to orbit Earth.

A trip to the moon was looking more and more possible.

John Glenn orbited Earth on February 20, 1962.

During testing, astronaut Edward White receives help from a technician.

PREPARATIONS

NASA had just nine years to meet President Kennedy's deadline. NASA officials identified more than 10,000 separate tasks that had to be accomplished to send an expedition to the moon. The to-do list included everything from designing and building the spacecraft to figuring out what astronauts could eat and wear. NASA had to map the moon, plan a route, and pick a landing site. They had to choose and train astronauts, make tools for collecting moon rocks, and test cameras for filming on the moon.

Just keeping a schedule of the project would be a huge challenge. NASA administrator Robert C. Seamans later wrote:

> *Each task had its particular objectives, its man power needs, its time schedule, and its complex interrelationship with many other tasks. Which had to be done first? Which could be done concurrently? What were the critical sequences?*[1]

In 1961, even the basic question of how to get to the moon was far from clear. The issue created a heated debate among NASA engineers. Three methods, or modes, presented themselves. In the first mode, a single rocket would shoot the astronauts all the way to the moon and back again.

Beloved Leader

As the Gemini program was getting underway, President John F. Kennedy was assassinated in Dallas on November 22, 1963. Many NASA workers were grief stricken over the death of the space program's biggest champion. Guards had to be posted around the Saturn rocket to keep employees from writing Kennedy's name on it as a tribute to their hero. Meanwhile, NASA officials worried about what would become of the space program without Kennedy. President Lyndon Johnson calmed the fears by making a strong symbolic gesture. Following his lead, the Department of the Interior changed the name of the location of NASA's launch center from Cape Canaveral to Cape Kennedy.

This method had the advantage of simplicity. However, such a massive rocket would be expensive and difficult to fly.

In the second mode, one spacecraft carrying the astronauts and another with fuel would be launched separately and put together in Earth's orbit. This method had the advantage of smaller rockets, but many feared the double launch would be too difficult to coordinate.

The third mode combined aspects of the first two. A single rocket would launch from Earth and the spacecraft would be divided into modules, or sections, based on their separate functions. The three modules were: the command module, where the astronauts piloted the spacecraft; the service module, which provided the command module's engine and fuel; and the lunar module, which was key to the design.

The lunar module was a special spacecraft designed just for landing on the moon. The single rocket would propel the astronauts all the way into orbit around the moon.

"I grew up on the farm working 16 hours a day, milking cows in the morning under 20 below zero. …To me, to know that I've been involved with one of the greatest achievements of mankind—I feel rather special about that."[2]

—*John Houbolt, the NASA engineer who came up with the idea of traveling to the moon by lunar module*

The lunar module was initially considered to be a very radical design

One astronaut would stay aboard the command module in lunar orbit while two others headed down to the surface of the moon in the lunar module. After the successful moon mission, the lunar module would carry the men back into lunar orbit, where they would meet up with the command module and return to Earth.

"Like many others, I initially thought this technique was dangerously complex, even bizarre," Aldrin later wrote in his memoirs.[3] Soon, though, the elegance of

"They were concerned on landing that when all of a sudden our hearts were pumping blood in [Earth's gravity], we might have problems. We'd pass out. Some of them thought we'd die. We never even got dizzy."[4]

—Gemini / astronaut
Frank Borman on
returning to Earth after
a record-breaking
14 days in space

the design became apparent. By July 1962, NASA was in agreement. The lunar module was the way to go.

Now the real work began. The lunar module required incredibly precise flying maneuvers that had never been performed. Could two spacecraft rendezvous, or meet up, in space while traveling at thousands of miles per hour and then join together?

NASA had other key questions as well. It would take over a week to travel to the moon and back. Could astronauts survive that long in space? What would be the effects of weightlessness? The astronauts would have to exit the spacecraft and walk on the moon. Could a spacesuit offer enough protection for a human being to survive in the vacuum of outer space?

More astronauts were chosen, and NASA began Project Gemini. These astronauts would answer as many of NASA's questions as they could while staying in Earth's orbit.

By 1965, NASA was moving forward on several fronts. Gemini astronauts were preparing to fly the nation's first two-man mission into space. Unmanned Ranger space probes were sending back thousands of close-up photos of the moon's surface. Some 20,000 U.S. companies were designing and building the spacecraft and equipment the space travel required, while NASA's staff swelled to 33,200 people.

Americans were finally beginning to feel like they were catching up in the space race. Then, in March, the familiar fear struck again. Soviet cosmonaut Alexei Leonov stepped out of his spacecraft and performed the first-ever space walk. For 12 minutes, he floated free in the blackness of space, his country's name proudly displayed across his space suit.

NASA had to catch up. In June, astronaut Ed White climbed out of the *Gemini 4* capsule with the American flag showing prominently across his left arm. Attached by a golden cord, he drifted from his spaceship. Below him, Earth's blue oceans shone, and clouds sparkled like snow drifts in the bright sun.

White's beaming face was not visible beneath his mirrored visor as he tumbled high above the skies. "I feel like a million dollars!" he exulted.[5] And Americans exulted upon his safe return. Postage stamps showing the space walker were soon pasted on letters all over the United States.

Project Gemini started to pick up speed. Each mission answered another question or proved another skill. In August, *Gemini 5* astronauts orbited Earth for eight days. The astronauts emerged from the longest time in space without any negative effects. Then, in December, *Gemini 7* extended the record to 14 days.

While *Gemini 7* flew 203 miles (326.6 km) above the Earth, the previously delayed *Gemini 6* blasted into space. It chased after *Gemini 7*. Soon both spacecraft were orbiting Earth at 25 times the speed of sound. Little by little, *Gemini 6* moved in toward *Gemini 7* until the two

Trail Blazers

As Gemini astronauts tested key maneuvers in Earth's orbit, unmanned probes shot to the moon. The goal for these probes was to answer questions such as: Is it even possible to land on the moon? At the time, scientists were not even sure if the moon was completely solid or just a dense ball of dust. If landing was possible, where was the best place to land? Three series of probes sent back information about the moon's geography and surface conditions.

In 1961, the Ranger probes were the first to shoot toward the moon. Just sending the probes all the way to the moon was enough of a challenge at this stage. The idea was that a probe would transmit as many pictures as possible before crashing into the moon. But even getting a probe to crash at its target proved difficult. It was not until *Ranger 7* that a probe actually sent images back to Earth. After two more successful probes, the Rangers sent back a total of 17,000 images of the lunar surface.

The next challenge was to create a probe that could land without crashing. Five Surveyor crafts made successful landings between June 1966 and January 1968. Robotic arms scooped up soil, while cameras sent back the first clear views of the lunar surface.

spacecraft were just a few feet away from each other.

It could be done! Now, if two spacecraft could dock, the necessary techniques for flying the lunar module would be demonstrated.

Gemini 8 was slated to perform the first "hard dock" in space with an unmanned rocket. The mission would require an exceptionally skilled pilot at the controls, an experienced flyer who could keep cool under pressure. NASA found just the astronaut, a 35-year old Ohio farm boy who had flown 78 combat missions in the Korean War almost 15 years earlier. His name was Neil Armstrong. His stunning performance on *Gemini 8* would prove to be a key factor in his selection as commander of the *Apollo 11* mission. As commander, he was assigned to be the first person to set foot on the moon.

In March 1966, *Gemini 8* tracked down its target. But just as Armstrong locked onto it, a thruster misfired

A Near Disaster

Ed White's historic space walk had created some breathtaking photos, but he had done little except drift around his spaceship. With *Gemini 9*, it was time to find out if an astronaut could actually perform work during a space walk. Finding the answer to that question nearly led to disaster. As astronaut Gene Cernan discovered, working in the vacuum of space was impossible with nothing to hold on to. He could move his arms and legs like a swimmer, but without water, he stayed in place. As Cernan struggled to gain control of his movements, his heart raced and his helmet faceplate began to fog over. During his two-hour space walk, the astronaut lost 10 pounds (4.5 kg) of sweat, and he barely managed to get back inside the spacecraft.

and the joined spacecraft started to spin wildly. Armstrong managed to break free from the rocket, but the misfiring thruster was on his craft. His spacecraft spun even more frantically out of control. Armstrong had to gain control of the ship before he and co-astronaut David Scott blacked out. Thinking quickly, Armstrong took over manual control of *Gemini 8*. He stabilized the craft and made an emergency landing.

In 20 months, the Gemini Program had launched ten Earth-orbiting missions. Together, Gemini astronauts had accomplished five space walks, ten rendezvous, and nine dockings. The program had answered all key questions and demonstrated every technique a moon flight required.

Now, a bigger question remained. Could a mission fly all the way to the moon and land there? It was time to start testing the actual spacecraft designed to make the historic flight. On January 27, 1967, the *Apollo 1* astronauts boarded their spacecraft to perform tests for the project's first mission. The day should have been one of routine testing and preparation. Instead, the day marks one of the greatest tragedies in the history of NASA.

Astronaut Ed White floating on a golden tether during his historic space walk

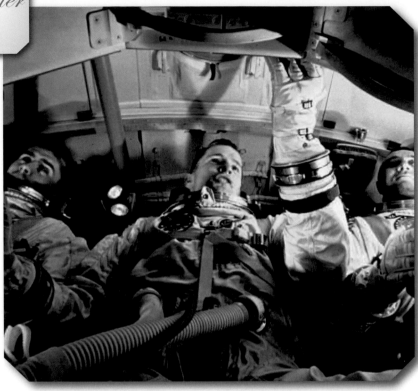

Astronauts Roger Chaffee, left, Ed White, center, and Virgil Grissom, the crew of Apollo I, during a practice session

TRIAL RUNS

The Gemini Program had been a huge success. But by January 1967, engineering problems with the first command module were causing several rounds of changes—and delays. Each change in the real spacecraft meant a corresponding one in the flight simulator used for training. By fall of 1966, the simulator had needed so many changes it was practically useless. *Apollo 1* commander Virgil "Gus" Grissom was fed up. To show his disgust, he hung a lemon over the simulator's hatch.

Grissom's co-astronauts were Ed White, the first American to perform a space walk, and Roger Chaffee. When the three men climbed aboard the command module on January 27, 1967, the last thing they wanted was another delay. After all, the men were there to take part in a simple countdown demonstration. To keep things moving, other tests would be performed at the same time. That meant the spacecraft would be filled with pure oxygen and the hatch would be sealed. The only way to open the hatch was from the outside, a procedure that would take technicians a full 90 seconds.

Soon after the three astronauts were squeezed inside the command module, it became clear that they were in for a long, frustrating procedure. The cabin stunk like sour milk, and there was so much static on the intercom that the astronauts could barely communicate

"... We are in a risky business, and we hope that if anything happens to us it will not delay the program. The conquest of space is worth the risk of life."[1]

—Apollo 1 *astronaut Virgil Grissom, shortly before he lost his own life during a test of the spacecraft in January 1967* with the technicians below. "How the hell can we get to the moon if we can't even talk between two buildings?" Grissom shouted over the static.[2]

The tests dragged on. For almost five-and-a-half hours, the men stayed sealed inside the tiny compartment in their bulky spacesuits. Then a terrifying scream came over the intercom from the command module.

Fire! ... We've got a fire in the cockpit! ... Let's get out! We're burning up! Get us out of here![3]

The men were sealed inside the burning cabin.

Astronaut Training

To prepare for the intense physical demands of space, the astronauts practiced "weightlessness" working underwater on mock spacecrafts. In the "boxing ring," they tried moving around on an extremely slippery surface.

If they could stomach it, flying in the "zero gravity" plane was more helpful. The plane flew in a steep up-and-down pattern, called parabolic loops. As the plane nosed downward, weightlessness could be achieved for about 30 seconds. Inside the padded plane, engineers and technicians stayed strapped down, while the astronauts floated freely. When the plane nosed up again, the men would be smacked against the floor.

"The wheel" prepared astronauts for the increased gravity they would feel during launch and re-entry to Earth. Sitting at the end of the wheel's 50-foot (15-m) metal arm, the astronaut would be spun around and around. The machine had the capacity to hit the rider with a force of 15 G's, or 15 times the normal force of gravity.

More enjoyable was training for moon gravity in the "Peter Pan rig." The astronauts were strapped into a contraption of pulleys and slings that offset five-sixths of their weight. They practiced jumping around as they later would along the moon's surface.

Technicians rushed to open the spacecraft, but flames surrounded the hatch. It took the crew a full five minutes to gain entry to the spacecraft. By then, it was far too late. In a pure oxygen environment, even aluminum burns. The spacecraft lay in ruins, and the *Apollo 1* astronauts were dead. "It was like a stomach punch for everyone in the program," remembered Glynn Lunney, NASA flight director. "And everybody no matter what role they had ... I think had a sense of guilt about it."[4]

NASA discovered the fire was probably sparked by faulty electrical wiring—disastrous in a sealed, pure oxygen environment. For almost two years, manned tests of the command module were put on hold while engineers thoroughly revised the spacecraft. In the end, they made 1,300 changes to the design—including a hatch that opened from inside the spacecraft in seven seconds.

All Up

Apollo 1 was costing the moon program months of necessary delay. It was time to test the *Saturn V* rocket. Two approaches could be taken. The entire rocket could be tested at once. Or, as the rocket engineers strongly suggested, it could be tested in stages, or parts. That way, problems could be more easily pinpointed. If anything went wrong, only one stage of the incredibly expensive rocket would be wasted. In the end, NASA administrators decided time was too precious. They would take their chances with an "all-up" test of the rocket. The rocket worked beautifully. And the all-up test saved millions of dollars and months of delays.

The charred Apollo I *interior after the flash fire that killed astronauts Roger Chaffee, Ed White, and Gus Grissom*

Apollo 1 was NASA's darkest hour. But NASA rose from the tragedy with a renewed commitment to finish what they had started. Later, many looked upon the tragedy with a bittersweet sense of gratitude. Rocco Petrone, NASA Director of Launch Operations, described the event:

> *I don't think we would have gotten to the moon in the*
> *'60s if we had not had the fire. If that had happened while*
> *we were on the way to the moon, we would have lost a crew,*
> *never heard from them again. It would have been a mystery*
> *hanging over the whole program, which would have caused*
> *an untold delay and maybe even a cancellation.*[5]

By October 1968, the program was back on track, and the first manned mission was launched. The goal of *Apollo 7* was to test out the command module and service module in Earth's orbit. The three Apollo astronauts successfully circled Earth for 11 days, and Americans were cheering NASA once again.

Next up was *Apollo 8*—the first mission to orbit the moon. Without the lunar module, the craft could not land or even test out rendezvous and docking. And yet the *Apollo 8* mission would provide a spectacular surprise. As *Apollo 8* shot far out of Earth's orbit and into the vastness of space, the astronauts were treated to an entirely new view of their home planet. In Earth orbit, the shimmering planet stretched beneath the spacecraft's windows like a distant ocean.

To astronaut Bill Anders, Earth looked "very delicate. ... [like] a Christmas tree ornament."[6]

During the Apollo 8 mission, astronaut Bill Anders took this photo, describing Earth as a delicate ornament.

"The vast loneliness up here ... is awe-inspiring," astronaut Jim Lovell said. "It makes you realize what you have back there on Earth."[7]

On December 24, 1968, the three astronauts became the first people to ever circle the moon. They had traveled thousands of miles farther from Earth than any previous astronauts. On that Christmas Eve, the men appeared on a live television broadcast. Almost one billion people in 64 countries watched as the astronauts took turns reading from the Bible. The story they read was from the *Book of Genesis*, and it described the biblical version of the creation of the universe.

The American public was seized with "go fever." Now that the "real" moon mission was so close, they realized the moon mission would be a reality. In January 1969, NASA announced the news that everyone had been waiting for. Who would fly *Apollo 11*, the first mission scheduled to actually land on the moon's surface? Neil Armstrong was appointed commander of the mission, and Buzz Aldrin would be the lunar module pilot. These two men would walk on the moon, while Michael Collins, command module pilot, would stay in the command module in lunar orbit.

The men were thrilled at their extraordinary fortune, but their future was not yet entirely sealed. In order for *Apollo 11* to land on the moon, the *Apollo 9* and *Apollo 10* missions had to go perfectly—and the lunar module was

"When I looked up and saw the Earth coming up on this very stark, beat-up lunar horizon, an Earth that was the only color that we could see—a very delicate-looking Earth—I was immediately almost overcome with the thought, 'You know, here we came all the way to the moon and yet the most significant thing we're seeing is our own home planet, the Earth.'"[8]

—*Bill Anders*, Apollo 8 astronaut

400,000 People

It took more than just astronauts and engineers to launch a rocket to the moon. Carpenters, plumbers, electricians, and welders were needed to make the designs come to life. Secretaries typed letters and answered phones. Others planned and packaged food. And someone needed to glue the layers of the astronauts' space suits. In all, Project Apollo created 400,000 jobs over 10 years.

still behind schedule. Then satellite photos revealed Soviet rockets enormous enough to power a spacecraft to the moon. Would the Soviets beat the United States after all?

In March 1969, *Apollo 9* launched with all three modules. The spacecraft operated flawlessly. By May, NASA was ready to perform a full dress rehearsal of the complete mission. The *Apollo 10* spacecraft went into moon orbit, and the lunar module descended toward the moon's surface. *Apollo 10* performed every key maneuver except one—they were not allowed to touch down on the moon's surface.

That privilege was reserved for *Apollo 11*. At last, a launch date could be set: July 16, 1969.

Earlier training done by the Apollo 8 crew and others paved the way for the Apollo 11 launch.

Blastoff during the Apollo 11 *launch*

Journey Through Space

On July 16, 1969, Armstrong, Aldrin, and Collins lifted off the launch pad at Cape Kennedy. In just a few seconds, the *Saturn V* rocket shot through the clouds and dust of Earth's atmosphere. The rocket continued to pick up speed. At one minute, five seconds after liftoff, the rocket broke the sound barrier, traveling at more than 738 miles per hour (1,188 km/h).

Armstrong, Aldrin, and Collins felt their bodies grow heavy. As the ride smoothed out, the men were pushed against their couches with a force of 4.5 G's, or 4.5 times the normal force of gravity. The

"There are two responses you can have when you first experience weightlessness—'Yahoo! This is great!' or 'Look out, I'm going to get seasick!'"[2]

—Charlie Duke of Apollo 16

sensation was similar to that of zooming upside down on a roller coaster. The men could barely lift their arms.

On later missions to the moon, the astronauts would cheer after a successful liftoff, but the mood on the Apollo 11 craft was serious. "All three of us are very quiet," Michael Collins would later write in his autobiography, "none of us seems to feel any jubilation at having left the earth, only a heightened awareness of what lies ahead."[1]

Three minutes into the flight, the Saturn V was hurtling toward outer space at more than 6,000 miles (9,656 km) per hour. Aboard Apollo 11, the men braced themselves for the rocket's first "staging." Saturn V was divided into three stages, or parts, that fired one after the other. The first stage was, by far, the largest. It had been responsible for taking the giant rocket safely out of Earth's atmosphere. Now at three minutes, five seconds, the stage's fuel was all used up. It was time for the stage to fall away.

Apollo 11 shook violently as explosives shot the first stage off. The 138-foot (42 m) piece of rocket would splash down into the Atlantic Ocean. Building on the momentum of the first stage, the smaller, second stage took over. In six minutes, it more than doubled the rocket's speed and altitude before it, too, was blasted off.

Now the third stage took over. Its first job was to propel the spacecraft into Earth's orbit. The idea was for the craft to circle Earth and pick up speed. Then the third stage would fire again, pushing the craft out of Earth's orbit and into its three-day journey toward the moon.

For two-and-a-half hours, Armstrong, Aldrin, and Collins coasted more than 100 miles (161 km) above Earth at a speed of more than 17,000 miles per hour. In one 88-minute orbit, the men saw a full cycle of day and night. They also experienced weightlessness, or microgravity. Though the pull of gravity exists in outer space, it is so minor that astronauts cannot feel it.

Shoppers stopping at televisions to watch the historic liftoff

Suddenly, the men could float around the cabin as if they truly were as light as balloons. Charlie Duke, an astronaut from a later Apollo mission, described weightlessness this way:

> *"Things feel sort of funny, and you unbuckle your seat belt and wiggle around in your seat or sort of tap your toes. … And all of a sudden, your body's just everywhere in the cabin, and you're doing flips and cartwheels and spins."*[3]

Suddenly there was no true "up" or "down." The astronauts could walk on the ceiling and look up at the floor. The cramped space felt roomier as the men gently bounced off the cabin's walls. Almost all astronauts experience nausea at the onset of weightlessness. But if the astronauts did have motion sickness, they did not have time to focus on their condition. While Earth glowed outside their window, the astronauts were in constant communication with Mission Control in Houston. Mission Control was a group of

Mission Control

While the three astronauts were traveling through space, another Earth-based crew was following their every move. The crew monitored the spacecraft's functions, its route, the astronaut's activities, and even their bodies. The Mission Control staff included fellow astronauts, computer technicians, scientists, and doctors. Their job was to make the mission as safe and successful as they possibly could.

Mission Control, or simply "Houston," communicated to the astronauts by radio. A network of tracking stations with giant antennas was stationed on land, ships, and aircrafts around the world. The tracking stations relayed messages between Houston and *Apollo 11*.

Houston provided the men with crucial information about their flight such as their position in space and instructions for key maneuvers.

As *Apollo 11* got farther and farther away from Mission Control, it took longer and longer for the voices from Houston to carry across the distance. The length of the silent gap before a response from Houston was an indicator and a reminder of how far the men had traveled. By the time Armstrong and Aldrin were landing on the moon, that gap was a full six seconds long.

astronauts, computer technicians, and other specialists who assisted the astronauts with practically every aspect of the flight. The astronauts kept busy checking systems, tracking their position, and preparing for "trans-lunar injection," or TLI, which meant leaving Earth orbit and coasting toward the moon.

Finally, word came from Mission Control—the crew was a go for TLI. Stage three fired again, pushing *Apollo 11* out of Earth orbit. The burn lasted four minutes, 45 seconds, before the engine turned off for good. The massive *Saturn V* rocket was completely spent, but very little rocket power was needed to complete the journey. In the vacuum of space, there was no air to slow the spacecraft. *Apollo 11* began its long coast to the moon.

Though the spacecraft had left Earth, its gravity still continued to influence the spacecraft's speed. As it traveled, *Apollo 11* would gradually slow down because of the diminishing effects of Earth's gravity. Then the craft would speed up as the moon's gravity "captured" it and drew it toward its ghostly surface. Meanwhile, the

Higher and Faster

Saturn V's engines were burning at a steady rate. Yet the higher the rocket traveled, the faster it went. Why? The rocket was rapidly losing weight, burning 2 million pounds (900,000 kg) of fuel a minute. The same force was soon lifting a spacecraft half its original weight. At the same time, wind resistance died away as the rocket escaped Earth's atmosphere.

No Twinkle

Outside the command module windows, thousands of stars shone in the blackness. However, these stars looked different from the way they are viewed from Earth. They did not twinkle. Why? The "twinkling" is actually light from the stars refracting, or bending, in Earth's atmosphere. Without air, there is no twinkle.

service module thrusters would provide power for any small turns that were required to keep *Apollo 11* on its correct path.

A few key maneuvers had to be performed before the men could take off their spacesuits, eat a meal, and relax. Collins carefully separated the command and service modules from the lunar module. He piloted them a short distance away, turned them completely around, and reconnected them to the lunar module—all while traveling at thousands of miles per hour. The lunar module was now connected to the "nose" of the bell-shaped command module, allowing passage from one vehicle to the other.

After the lunar module was connected, stage three of the rocket could be let go. Stage three was sent into solar orbit, to be burned up by the sun.

The last maneuver was to put the spacecraft in "barbecue" mode. The astronauts sent the spacecraft slowly spinning like a chicken roasting on a spit—and for much the same purpose. The "thermal roll" would give all sides of the craft equal exposure to the burning sun, regulating its temperature. This was to prevent fuel tanks from getting too hot and exploding and also to keep radiators from freezing.

At five hours, 15 minutes into the flight, the crew were ready for their first meal. They reached for their color-coded plastic pouches. The pouches had been labeled with the time and date of when they were to be eaten. They also had instructions for preparation. The astronauts' first meal was beef and potatoes. The men would not know it just by looking at the freeze-dried granules. Packet instructions told them how much water to add to reconstitute the entrée. Most astronauts agree that the food tasted bland. The eating experience, however, was anything but. In zero gravity, a spoonful of soup turned into a sparkling, floating ball.

Though they were traveling at an incredible speed, they could not feel it. There was no sense of motion traveling through the vacuum of space. There were no clear landmarks, either. Computers aboard the spacecraft and at Mission Control indicated *Apollo 11's* progress. So far from Earth, there also was no sunrise or sunset to mark the passing of the day. The men went to bed according to a strict schedule. Fourteen hours into the mission, they fastened covers on the windows and began their seven-hour "night." Armstrong and

Weightlessness Causes Weightiness?

Some Apollo astronauts were known to gain as much as a pound a day during the journey to the moon. As their heart rates slowed due to weightlessness, so did their metabolisms. Their bodies were not using up as many calories as they usually did. That, combined with lack of exercise, made some astronauts pack on the pounds—even in spite of the unappetizing packets of food.

Aldrin wriggled into mesh hammocks in two sleeping compartments, while Collins stretched out on the couches.

The next day, the men felt groggy after a fitful night. The astronauts' bodies were still adjusting to weightlessness. Their hearts did not have to work as hard pumping blood against gravity, so their heart rates had slowed down. The men likely felt weak or even light-headed. But during a television broadcast from the spacecraft later in the day, they tried not to show their fatigue. They were calm and businesslike as they took viewers on a tour of the craft and showed them their view of Earth.

Throughout the journey, the astronauts were in constant contact with Mission Control. Inside the command module a constellation of 600 gauges, dials, control switches, and circuit breakers required frequent monitoring. Sixty-three hours into the flight, the extraterrestrials were captured by the moon's gravitational pull. *Apollo 11* began to speed up. It was almost time to enter lunar orbit.

The Apollo 11 crew would leave behind this plaque to commemorate their visit.

Buzz Aldrin descending the steps of the Lunar Module

Moon Landing

s Collins later wrote, the astronauts saw the all-important entry into the moon's orbit as the true beginning of the mission. "All of us are aware that the honeymoon is over and we are about to lay our little pink bodies on the line."[1] The men were acutely aware of the risk. They had just one shot at "lunar orbit insertion," or LOI—and this one chance had to take place with split-second accuracy. If *Apollo 11's* crew missed their chance, they would hurtle past the moon and on toward the outer edges of the solar system with a limited oxygen supply and no hope of return.

"I marvel again at the precision of our path. We have missed hitting the moon by a paltry 300 nautical miles, at a distance of nearly a quarter of a million miles from Earth, and don't forget that the moon is a moving target."[3]

—*Michael Collins*

To further heighten the stakes, LOI had to take place on the "dark side" of the moon. Only one side of the moon's sphere ever faces Earth. During its passage over the dark side of the moon, *Apollo 11* would be out of radio contact with Mission Control. The astronauts would have to perform LOI completely on their own.

> Apollo 11, *this is Houston. All your systems are looking good going around the corner. ... We'll see you on the other side.*[2]

As *Apollo 11* rounded the moon and entered its shadow, the astronauts were treated to their first good look at the moon. Before darkness took over, the blinding glare of the sun was replaced by a much more welcome light—the soft glow of "earthshine."

The men were overcome with the moon's mysterious beauty. "The view of the moon that we've been having recently is really spectacular," Armstrong told Mission Control. "It fills about three quarters of the hatch window. … It's a view worth the price of the trip."[4]

But there was not much time for moon gazing. Collins now had to perform the maneuver he had been nervously anticipating. The spacecraft was traveling too fast to stay in lunar orbit, so Collins turned it around. The exhaust nozzles were now facing the direction they were traveling. When Collins flicked on the service module's engines, they acted as brakes.

For the first time in three days, the astronauts felt the power of the spacecraft. They slammed against their couches as *Apollo 11* seemed to dive straight into the moon. For five minutes, 59 seconds, the engines burned while the moon rapidly filled the command module windows. Then the firing stopped. LOI had been successful. *Apollo 11* drifted out from the far side of the moon into the blinding light of lunar noon—and back into communication with a relieved crew at Mission Control.

The next major operation would be to separate the lunar module from the command module to prepare for a landing. Before then, the astronauts would circle

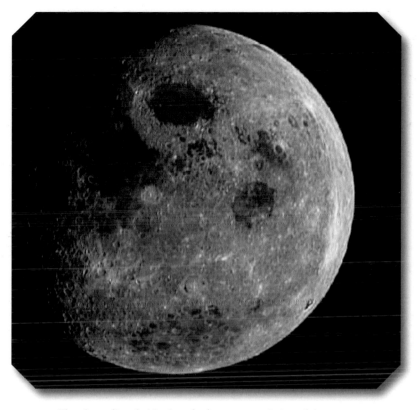

*The glow of "earthshine" made the astronauts' view of the moon
even more spectacular.*

the moon 11 more times, preparing the lunar module
and fine-tuning their path and landing approach.

   With each two-hour orbit around the moon, the
astronauts examined its surface. They were surprised at
how rocky and rough it looked—including the landing
site, the Sea of Tranquility. The "sea" was really a
desert-like flatland and had been selected for that

reason. Up close, however, the Sea of Tranquility looked distressingly full of craters and boulders.

After 20 hours of circling the moon, the time had come for the two crafts to separate. Armstrong and Aldrin climbed into the lunar module, which now had the new name *Eagle*, after the U.S. national symbol. While Armstrong and Aldrin landed on the moon, Collins was assigned to continue piloting the command module *Columbia* in lunar orbit. After a successful moon landing, the *Eagle* would fly back up to *Columbia*. The two spacecraft would dock and the threesome would

The Lunar Module

Stepping into the lunar module, an astronaut faced the cabin's opposite wall just three-and-a-half feet (1 m) away. From the outside, the entire spacecraft was just 22 feet (6.7 m) tall and 31 feet (9.4 m) across. And yet this tiny spacecraft would serve as the moon lander, the astronaut's base camp for 22 hours, and the moon launcher.

The spacecraft was so small because it had to be extremely light in order to fly. Its more than one million parts could not weigh more than 4.3 tons (3.9 metric tons). Engineers looked to cut excess weight everywhere they could. Seats were some of the first items to go. This saved the weight of the seats themselves and also allowed for a smaller "windshield." The pilot would stand right up against the small, triangular window as they landed. Another weight saver was the paper-thin aluminum hull. Even toothbrushes and soap were too heavy. The astronauts would have to make do without such luxuries.

The lunar module looked a lot less like an eagle and much more like another nickname, the "bug." Because there is no air resistance on the moon, engineers did not have to create a streamlined, bullet-shaped vehicle. The result was a rounded, lumpy structure on long, spindly legs.

return together to Earth in the command module.

Aldrin and Armstrong sealed the hatch of the *Eagle*. Collins threw a release switch, and explosives blasted the lunar module away.

"The *Eagle* has wings!"[5]

Collins radioed to his crewmembers, "You guys take care."

"See you later," Armstrong replied.[6] It was a promise the world was waiting for him to keep.

The *Eagle* was less than three hours away from touching down on the surface of the moon. However, to the two astronauts and the crew at Mission Control, the last few minutes of those few hours would feel like days.

Keeping Expectations Low

All three men were nervous as landing day approached. Of the three men, however, Collins was the most expressive, as was later demonstrated by his often poetic retelling of the events in his autobiography, *Carrying the Fire*. He made the following wry remark about landing day: "If we were bullfighters, we would call it the moment of truth, but all I want is a moment of no surprises."[7]

The first sign of trouble came as Armstrong noticed that an important landmark, the Maskelyne W crater, flashed in his window two seconds too early. The *Eagle* was coming in too fast and was going to overshoot the intended landing site. Mission Control assessed the situation and gave the men the go-ahead to continue.

Mission Control closely followed the Apollo 11 *crew and the* Eagle's *landing.*

Just moments later an alarm sounded from the *Eagle's* computer. "It's a 1202," Aldrin reported.[8]

What was that? Ground technicians frantically searched the codebook to find the meaning of this obscure alarm. At last they found it; 1202 was an "executive overflow." The computer was alerting the pilots that it was overloaded. Why? No one knew for sure, but Mission Control gave the go-ahead to proceed.

The *Eagle's* engines continued their powered descent, acting as brakes to slow the spacecraft and save it from a crash landing.

Then another alarm flashed. "1201," Aldrin shouted.[9] Another computer overload. Once again, Mission Control overrode the computer warning and gave the go for landing.

Meanwhile, an alarming sight was passing outside the *Eagle's* windows. It looked as though the men were headed straight for a huge crater filled with boulders.

The *Eagle's* computer could no longer be trusted. Armstrong grabbed the red-handled joystick to manually land the spacecraft. He turned the *Eagle* sideways to look for a new landing site, taking the mission even farther off course and at the expense of precious fuel.

The "descent fuel" supply was of utmost concern. While the lunar module was equipped with fuel for both landing (descent) and take off, the two supplies were completely separate. If Armstrong used up the descent fuel, the *Eagle* would crash. If the two men did not die from the crash itself, they would die from leaks in the thin aluminum hull of their aircraft. Exposure to the harsh moon environment would be equally deadly.

Still Human, After All

Armstrong was well known for keeping his cool under pressure. In his career as a test pilot and astronaut, he had faced life-threatening situations before. And during the launch of the *Saturn V* rocket on July 16, medical equipment attached to his body had read his heartbeat at just 115 beats per minute. During the moon landing, however, his heart was racing at 156 beats per minute. Later, when he was told about his racing heart, he remarked, "I'd be really disturbed with myself if it hadn't."[13]

At 200 feet (61 m) above the moon, Armstrong found a landing spot. He turned the *Eagle* into landing position.

"Sixty seconds." Mission Control warned the men that only one minute's worth of fuel remained.[10] The *Eagle* slowly drifted down. Soon Armstrong and Aldrin could not see anything out their window. They were completely engulfed in moon dust kicked up by their engines.

"Thirty seconds." Mission Control warned again.[11]

A few seconds later, the astronauts felt a slight bump. "Contact light!" Aldrin shouted.

"We copy you down, *Eagle*." It was 3:18 p.m. Houston time on July 20, 1969.

"Houston, Tranquility Base here. The *Eagle* has landed," Armstrong said.

"Roger, Tranquility. We copy you on the ground. You've got a bunch of guys about to turn blue. We're breathing again. Thanks a lot."[12]

The lunar module's descent to the moon, seen here, was a success.

Astronaut Buzz Aldrin walks on the moon.

ONE GIANT LEAP

What would it be like to stand on the moon? Armstrong and Aldrin had arrived at the most foreign—and most hostile—environment humans had ever encountered. Here was a desert more barren than any on Earth, a dry, rocky wasteland of stark, foreboding beauty. Here was a vastness, empty of water, air, and life. Here was a land where tiny flying shards of dust—micrometeoroids— could shred one's skin.

Without air, there was no wind, no life-giving oxygen, no air pressure to keep the body's lungs from exploding and the blood from bubbling. Without air's moderating influence, temperatures on the moon hit both extremes. In sunlight, it would be blistering hot. Stepping into a shadow, though, an astronaut would face instant, polar cold. Without air molecules, there was no medium to carry sound vibrations. If it were not for the radio headsets inside their helmets, the astronauts would not hear a single sound on the moon.

Without air, the moon's sky is a permanent ink-black, even with the sun blazing overhead. Apollo astronauts would discover that being on the moon during "daylight" was like standing in the middle of a floodlit football stadium at night. The lack of air also made it difficult to get

Stiff Suit

In their bulky space suits, the astronauts could not simply bend down and pick up rock samples. The suit was too stiff to easily bend, and the astronauts could not risk falling over. Maybe they would not be able to get back up or— even worse—they could tear their suits and leak precious oxygen into space. So instead of bending, the men used a specially designed tool that was a long metal pole with a shovel at the bottom.

What Color Is the Moon?

Apollo astronauts have had a hard time reporting on the ever-changing colors of the moon's surface. Past one's shadow, moon soil looks bright like snow. Off to the sides of one's shadow, however, it can be light grey, dark grey, or tan. On an astronaut's space suit, moon dust looks like powdered charcoal.

one's bearings. With no dusty air interfering with the view, even faraway objects look sharp and focused. That, combined with the close horizon of the smaller sphere, made it hard for the astronauts to judge distance.

The astronauts spent several hours inside the *Eagle* preparing for their exit. They had to depressurize their cabin before opening the hatch. They also had to put on their Extravehicular Mobility Units (EMUs), or space suits, for walking on the moon. In addition to the layers they had already worn, the EMUs had an extra outer layer for protection against extreme temperatures and micrometeoroids. The EMUs came equipped with high-tread boots to tackle the moon's dusty surface. The unit included a life-giving backpack with nearly four hours worth of oxygen. On Earth, an EMU weighed 180 pounds (82 kg), but the moon's gravity was one-sixth that of Earth's. To the astronauts, the spacesuit felt like 30 pounds (14 kg).

Finally, almost seven hours after the contact light went off, Armstrong prepared to open the *Eagle's* hatch. Carefully and methodically, he began to climb down

The world watched as Neil Armstrong took the first steps on the moon.

the nine rungs of the *Eagle's* ladder. On his way, he activated the TV camera mounted on the spacecraft. About one-seventh of all people in the world were waiting to catch sight of the first person ever to walk on the moon. For the rest of their lives, each would be able to report exactly where they were and what they were doing when they saw Neil Armstrong walk on the moon. On grainy, black-and-white TV screens, a bulky white figure stood out against the black moon sky.

Armstrong reported:

> I'm at the foot of the ladder. [T]he surface appears to be very, very fine grained as you get close to it. It's almost like a powder. … I'm going to step off the LM [lunar module] now.[1]

It was 9:56 p.m., Houston time, in the evening of July 20, 1969. Neil Armstrong had planted his boot onto the moon's dusty surface.

> That's one small step for a man, one giant leap for mankind.[2]

During his next few steps, Armstrong proved that he would not sink in the dust. He would not fall over from the weight of his backpack, and,

Michael Collins' Solitary Vigil

What was Michael Collins doing during the 22 hours that Aldrin and Armstrong were on the moon? He was orbiting the moon every two hours aboard the command module, waiting for his fellow astronauts' safe return.

Before the astronauts left on their historic journey, many people had expressed sympathy for Collins. After all, he was the one who did not get to actually walk on the moon. During a pre-launch press conference, Collins informed the public that he did not feel slighted at all in his role as command module pilot.

As he kept his solitary vigil, Collins was treated to a completely new view of the universe. When in the shadow of the moon, the moon was just a black circle where no stars were shining. As he emerged, he first saw the moon illuminated by the Earth's soft blue glow. Then he flew into brilliant sunlight as he passed into lunar noon.

Collins later wrote that his "secret terror" was that his fellow astronauts would get stranded on the moon, and Collins would have to fly back to Earth alone.

indeed, walking on the moon was not a problem. In fact, as the astronauts got used to it, walking on the moon seemed more fun than walking on Earth. The astronauts could take long, bouncing steps or hop forward on both legs like a kangaroo.

After getting his bearings, Armstrong took photos and collected rock samples. He looked around, remarking that the moon "has a stark beauty all its own. It's like much of the high desert of the United States. It's different, but it's very pretty out here."[3]

About 15 minutes later, Aldrin joined Armstrong. The men looked at the checklists posted on their puffy wrists and got back to work. They still had 50 pounds of moon rocks to collect. They also set up three experiments. As Armstrong later noted, the greatest difficulty was not temperatures, or gravity, or the EMU. "The primary difficulty that we observed was that there was just far too little time to do the variety of things that we would have liked to have done."[4]

A Fitful Night

Still wearing their bulky space suits, Armstrong and Aldrin tried to get a night's sleep aboard the lunar module before taking off. In the tiny spacecraft, there was no place to actually lie down, and the cabin was too cool for sleeping. While Aldrin tried to curl up on the floor, Armstrong rested semi-upright in a hammock between the engine cover and a support. If that was not uncomfortable enough, Armstrong had another distraction to deal with. His head was up against an uncovered window where Earth shone down on him like "a big blue eyeball."[5]

Timeless Footprints

Buzz Aldrin accidentally took a photo of a footprint of his boot that has since become one of the most famous images of the times. Because there is no wind or water on the moon, there is no erosion. That footprint, like all the others left by the Apollo astronauts, will stay intact for 500,000 years. That is how long it will take for micrometeoroids, or flying dust, to wear the footprint away.

Plus Armstrong and Aldrin had a number of ceremonial duties scheduled. The first was unveiling a plaque on the lunar module that would be left on the moon, which read: Here men from the planet Earth first set foot on the Moon, July 1969 A.D. We came in peace for all mankind.

That idea—peace for all mankind—was a theme that ran behind all the ceremonies performed on the moon. As the astronauts planted a U.S. flag in the moon's soil, Mission Control interrupted them with a special request. President Richard Nixon was calling from the White House:

> ... [A]s you talk to us from the Sea of Tranquility, it inspires us to redouble our efforts to bring peace and tranquility to Earth.[6]

Two hours and 14 minutes after the "giant leap," it was time for the astronauts to return to the *Eagle*. As Aldrin and Armstrong climbed back on board, they knew one untested maneuver was left—flying the *Eagle* off the surface of the moon.

A footprint left by one of the astronauts shows in the soft, powdery surface of the moon.

The Apollo 11 lunar module, the Eagle, rises from the moon's surface to dock with Columbia and return to Earth.

BACK TO EARTH

For most of the flight's key maneuvers, the engineers had built back-up measures. If one engine did not fire, another would take over. But the lunar module had to be so light, the engineers did away with that safety feature. The astronauts had just one chance to take off from the moon on a single ascent engine. If anything went wrong, they would be stranded there forever. Furthermore, take-off from the moon was one of the few key operations that had never previously been tested. How could it?

"[Y]ou're cleared for takeoff," Mission Control informed the men standing by inside the *Eagle*.

"Roger, understand," Aldrin replied. Then, he joked, "We're Number One on the runway."[1]

The *Eagle's* engine fired, and the stages of the lunar module violently separated. The ascent stage streaked upward, while the descent stage served as its launch pad. Three minutes later, the *Eagle* was hurtling upward at 1,000 miles (1,600 km) per hour. The next challenge was to get into lunar orbit and rendezvous with *Columbia*.

About four hours after take-off, the two spacecraft were locked together once again, and the crew was reunited. The astronauts still had 240,000 miles (386,000 km) to go and at least two more major hurdles, but they rejoiced at being together.

A Good Strategy

Outwardly, at least, Armstrong did not seem worried about the grim possibility of becoming stranded on the moon. When asked about it during a pre-launch press conference, he dismissed it, saying, "That's an unpleasant thing to think about. We've chosen not to think about that at the present time. We don't think that's a likely situation. It's simply a possible one. At the present time, we're left with no recourse should that occur."[2]

Slow Trip Home

The return home from any trip may seem to drag on, but in the case of *Apollo 11*, that feeling was based somewhat in reality. The astronauts could not feel motion, but they knew that until they were "captured" by Earth's gravity, they were traveling slowly by space standards. Indeed, day one of the return trip would take them just 5,000 miles (8,000 km). By the end of the second day, they would go another 35,000 miles (56,000 km). Then, by day three, they were in Earth's "sphere of influence," making up the final 200,000 miles (320,000 km) of the trip in just one day.

The crew filled the *Eagle* with used equipment and supplies, and the spacecraft was blasted off the command module. The *Eagle* would stay in orbit about the moon for several months before it would crash into the moon's surface.

Next came another potentially deadly maneuver—getting out of lunar orbit, or "trans-Earth injection" (TEI). Like the ascent from the surface, the astronauts had just one shot. They had to fire, or "burn," the engine on the service module, increasing speed in order to leave lunar orbit and head toward Earth. If the burn failed, the crew faced two gruesome options. They would either be shot into outer space, or they would be fated to forever orbit the moon—with just five-day's worth of oxygen.

For the last time, the spacecraft rounded the dark side of the moon. Collins flipped the switch, and, for three minutes, the men experienced one of the trip's few sensations of motion. Soon the crew shot around the front of the moon. Only this time, they kept going.

TEI had been successful. As the men watched the moon shrink outside their window, they settled in for the long journey back. Soon enough, however, the boredom would be interrupted with another wild ride—reentering Earth's atmosphere. The spacecraft would approach the Earth's atmosphere at incredible speeds. The spacecraft had to enter at just the right angle. If it came in too steep, the astronauts would skip off the atmosphere like a stone off water. If they did not come in steep enough, they would be shot back into outer space with no hope of return.

The reentry angle had to be accurate to within half a degree. As *Apollo 8* astronaut Bill Anders put it, the target was comparable to "about the size of a letter slot seen four miles away."[3]

As *Apollo 11* reached Earth's atmosphere, the service module was blasted off. The monstrous rocket and spacecraft from launch day was now reduced to the 9-foot (2.7-m) command module. Of the original 7.5 million pounds (3.4 million kg), only 11,000 pounds (5,000 kg) remained. It was all that was needed. Air friction would serve as the brakes.

Coming in at 25,000 miles (40,000 km) per hour—32 times the speed of sound—*Apollo 11* tore into

Earth's atmosphere. As anticipated, the heat shield started to burn off. The astronauts could see chunks of it flying past their window. Outside temperatures reached 5,000 degrees Fahrenheit (2,700° C) while inside temperatures peaked at 80 degrees Fahrenheit (27° C). *Apollo 11* was falling out of the sky. The last hurdle had been passed.

At 10,000 feet (3,000 m), the astronauts' bodies felt like lead as they were pushed against their couches with a force of 6.5 G's. The module's three red-and-white striped parachutes had been deployed, filling with air.

Life after *Apollo 11*

"Being an astronaut is a tough act to follow," Michael Collins wrote in his autobiography.[4]

Shortly after their return to Earth, the astronauts became instant celebrities. In Neil Armstrong's typical, reserved way, he avoided the public spotlight as much as possible. For a time he was a professor of aerospace engineering. In 1986, Armstrong was briefly in the limelight again. He helped lead a committee of experts to investigate the cause of the *Challenger* space shuttle explosion. He then continued his career in private business.

Of the three, Buzz Aldrin had the hardest time adjusting to his new life on Earth. "I had gone to the moon. What to do next? What possible goal could I add now?" he later wrote.[5] The astronaut struggled with depression while his personal life shattered around him. The experience led him to write his first autobiography *Return to Earth*, published in 1973. Aldrin has gone on to contribute to or co-author several books about space topics.

Collins had decided that the mission would be his last. In 1971, he became the curator of the Smithsonian Institute's National Air and Space Museum in Washington, D.C. During that time, he published his first autobiography, *Carrying the Fire*, in 1974. He then went on to work as a private aerospace consultant and freelance writer.

After 14 more minutes of falling, the singed, ravaged spacecraft splashed into the Pacific Ocean off the coast of Hawaii. Collins activated the command module's flotation bags, and the spacecraft bobbed like a dinghy in the ocean waves. It was 12:50 p.m. on July 24, 1969. The men were back on Earth's surface for the first time since the elevator ride up the launch tower eight days earlier. The mission had been a resounding success. The astronauts were safe. They were more than safe. They were heroes.

Though the men had just returned from the journey of their lifetimes, it would still be 17 days before they were able to hug their families or talk to them face-to-face. That was the length of the required quarantine. The astronauts would spend nearly three weeks in a special laboratory separated from almost all other people. They would stay there until it was clear that they had not carried back any strange moon diseases.

More Than Just Three Men

During the astronauts' TV appearance during the homebound trip, Armstrong addressed the American public, saying, "The responsibility for this flight lies first with history and with the giants of science who have preceded this effort. Next, with the American people, who have, through their will, indicated their desire. Next, to the four [presidential] administrations and their Congresses for implementing that will. … We would like to give a special thanks to all those Americans who built those spacecraft, who did the construction, design, the tests, and put their hearts and all their abilities into those craft."[6]

Mice Indicators

"Keep the mice healthy," Collins had jokingly said to Mission Control as *Apollo 11* ended its journey home.[8] He was referring to the army of rodents that was standing by. The plan was to feed the animals crushed moon rocks and then observe them. If the mice became strangely ill, then NASA would have plenty to worry about. Luckily, it turned out that neither astronauts nor mice caught any moon diseases.

Soon two rescue teams arrived to pull the men out of the spacecraft. The rescue workers disinfected the spacecraft's hatch and then opened it. The men's bodies were no longer used to Earth's gravity, and their limbs felt stiff and heavy as they climbed out. Armstrong, Aldrin, and Collins put on special suits called "biological isolation garments" (BIGs), which they would wear to the quarantine facilities. A helicopter carried them to the aircraft carrier that would take them back to land.

President Richard Nixon was waiting there to greet them. He spoke to them through the window of the Mobile Quarantine Facility:

> … [A]s a result of what you have done, the world has never been closer together before. We just thank you for that. … We can reach for the stars just as you have reached so far for the stars.[7]

The astronauts had just completed a strange, marvelous journey. But more uncharted territory lay ahead.

The Apollo 11 crew in the isolation unit after splashdown and recovery

Later Apollo missions included newer technologies and tools, such as the Lunar Roving Vehicle.

LATER MISSIONS

*I*t seemed as if everyone on Earth was celebrating the success of *Apollo 11*. Even the government-controlled Soviet newspaper reported, "We rejoice at the success of the American astronauts."[1] What started as fear had grown into a symbol of peace.

The United States had won the space race. However, NASA was still planning on sending nine more Apollo missions. Now that beating the Russians was no longer a factor, what would be the point of future trips to the moon?

Each new mission would take the astronauts to new moon territory, and with each mission, the astronauts would stay longer on the moon's surface. During *Apollo 12*, the goal was to perform a pinpoint moon landing—with no computer alarms—and recover pieces of a nearby lunar probe. By the last missions, astronauts were staying three days on the moon, performing seven-hour excursions on the lunar surface. The astronauts brought new tools and more advanced experiments.

As the threat of the Russians faded into memory and the challenge of getting on the moon was overcome, science became the new goal of Project Apollo. But for

Fun on the Moon

Neil Armstrong's first steps on the moon were solemn and cautious. As moon landings became more routine, other astronauts let their enthusiasm show. *Apollo 12* astronauts sang and joked while they worked. *Apollo 14*'s Alan Shepard attached the head of a golf club to one of the scientific tools. In his bulky suit, he was able to swing one-handed at a golf ball that, he joked, went "miles and miles" on the moon's gravity.[2] While saluting the American flag, *Apollo 16*'s John Young gleefully jumped several feet in the air while Charlie Duke snapped his photo.

Moon Grenades

In one moon experiment, mortars fired bombs into the lunar vacuum. The bombs exploded upon crashing into the ground, sending shockwaves vibrating several hundreds of miles across the lunar surface. Moonquake detectors then "read" the shockwaves. Because waves travel differently through different substances, the experiment provided clues about what the moon is made of.

many Americans, this new goal—science—was not compelling enough to justify the expense of more moon trips. On college campuses, protests against the Vietnam War were at their height. As American troops were dying overseas, Armstrong's first steps were losing their power to inspire. By 1971, the last three Apollo missions had been cut. There would be just six more missions after *Apollo 11*, ending in *Apollo 17*.

One of those missions, *Apollo 13*, would never make it to the moon's surface, and yet it would be regarded as a miraculous success. In April 1970, the world's attention was once again riveted by a trip to the moon.

Just nine minutes after signing off from a television session while en route to the moon, the astronauts of *Apollo 13* heard a loud, muffled bang outside their spacecraft. Then a second blast shook the spacecraft. Their oxygen supply was streaming out into space! With new procedures generated on the fly by Mission Control, the astronauts were able to coax the damaged ship around the moon and return safely to Earth.

The cause of the explosion was soon identified. Damaged wiring resulted in a spark that caused an oxygen tank to explode. Though easily corrected, the error was significant. It was now up to *Apollo 14* to renew the nation's faith in NASA and the moon program. Blasting off in January 1971, *Apollo 14* headed to where *Apollo 13* was to have gone, the Fra Mauro highlands. Alan Shepard, America's first astronaut in space, was in command.

This was to be the program's first true science mission. One of the key assignments was to collect samples from Cone Crater, where some of the moon's oldest rocks were thought to be located. But Shepard and fellow astronaut Ed Mitchell never made it there. They became disoriented by the uniform terrain and the inability to judge distances on the lunar surface. They ended up turning around just as they were approaching their target.

Scientists were disappointed in *Apollo 14*, but the mission had been a technical success. It was safe to go to the moon again. As NASA planned for the next missions, they focused on science. How could they make the most of the final three moon landings?

The final three missions would land in rugged terrain, by mountains, craters, and canyons that held more promise for finding interesting geological samples. The lunar module was redesigned to accommodate a longer stay. Now the astronauts could take off their space suits for sleeping in comfortable hammocks.

The most dramatic improvement of the final missions was the lunar rover, a vehicle designed for operating in the moon's low gravity. Riding in the lunar module, astronauts from *Apollo 15* were able to cover 16 miles (25 km). They collected 170 pounds (77 kg) of samples, nearly twice as much as *Apollo 14*. One of those

Lunar Rover

The engineers of the universe's first moon cars faced a daunting challenge—designing a vehicle with amazing ability but of extremely low weight. The lunar rover would have to maneuver flawlessly over the moon's rugged terrain. It would contain its own navigation system as well as devices for radio and TV communication with Earth. It had to operate in a 500-degree Fahrenheit (260° C) temperature range and in a vacuum. Plus it had to fold up like a lawn chair to fit inside the space of a small trunk.

In 17 months, the engineers had matched the challenge. The topless two-seater with its umbrella-like antenna looked more like a golf cart than a space-age miracle. However, the lunar rover was just what the mission required.

Built mostly of aluminum, the lunar rover weighed just 471 pounds (214 kg). The vehicle's wheels were made of wire mesh that rolled effortlessly over the moon's dusty surface. The astronauts steered the rover with a joystick. In moon's low gravity, a bump could send them sailing through space. During their stops, they pointed the TV antenna toward Earth, and Houston could look over the astronaut's shoulders while they worked. During *Apollo 15*, clear, full-color images from the lunar rover were broadcast live on television.

samples was the white "genesis" rock. Dating back 4.5 billion years, the rock was essentially as old as the moon itself.

The nation barely seemed to notice the *Apollo 16* mission, though the astronauts stayed even longer on the lunar surface and collected even more samples.

On December 7, 1972, the last mission of Project Apollo blasted into the night sky at Cape Canaveral. Crowds gathered to watch a moon launch one last time. They bid farewell not only to *Apollo 17* but also to the entire project and to an age of moon wonder.

On board was the first-ever scientist astronaut. Jack Schmitt was a trained geologist, and this was his one chance to find evidence of the moon's volcanic past. *Apollo 17* landed by the Taurus Mountains and Littrow Crater near the dark side of the moon. During a total of 22 hours of

Life After the Moon Landings

Of all 24 Apollo astronauts, only one continued to be a space pilot after his Apollo flight. Many went on to become successful businessmen with companies dealing in aerospace and related technology. Others embarked on the following professions:

President of an airline (Frank Borman, *Apollo 8*)

Three-star Air Force general (Tom Stafford, *Apollo 10*)

Painter (Alan Bean, *Apollo 12*)

Executive vice president of a pro football team (Dick Gordon, *Apollo 12*)

Founded a ministry (Jim Irwin, *Apollo 15*)

U.S. senator from New Mexico (Jack Schmitt, *Apollo 17*)

TV journalist (Gene Cernan, *Apollo 17*)

Dangerous Dust

Apollo 17's lunar rover accidentally lost its rear fender. Without its protection, the two astronauts were showered with moon dust while they drove, turning their gleaming white space suits dark grey. The astronauts had to clean their suits immediately. In the intense glare of the sun, a dark suit would roast the man inside. The astronauts tried to brush each other off, but the jagged dust worked its way into the suit's threads. The fender would simply have to be replaced. Mission Control worked all night on a solution. The answer? Use duct tape and a laminated map to make a replacement fender. The new part worked great, and the mission was saved.

moon excursions, Schmitt found what he came for—a patch of orange soil among the endless gray. The soil was evidence that lava had once flowed on the moon.

In addition to scientific discoveries, the *Apollo 17* astronauts were treated to breathtaking views of the moon. *Apollo 17* commander Gene Cernan knew he would be the last person to witness the moon's haunting landscape for a long time. At last, it was time to climb inside. Cernan said,

As I take man's last step from the surface, back home for some time to come … I believe history will record that America's challenge of today has forged man's destiny of tomorrow. And as we leave the moon at Taurus–Littrow, we leave as we came, and, God willing, as we shall return, with peace and hope for all mankind.[3]

Apollo 17 *crewmen found orange soil on the last moon mission.*

The moon orbiting Earth

MOON LEGACY

There are many ways to remember landing on the moon. Most remember the wonder at Armstrong's now-famous words making their way from the distant moon to their living rooms. The wonder was so powerful that even the Soviets rejoiced with

Americans on humanity's shared accomplishment. The Cold War was the spark for Project Apollo. And yet, the Apollo astronauts tread on the moon's surface with great humility. Gazing at the blue ball of Earth above them, they spoke words of peace—not victory.

"If we can land a man on the moon, we can do anything!" was the sentiment among Americans at the time. It was a thought that made people feel almost giddy with possibilities. But for some, including many black Americans fighting for civil rights, the feeling that "we can do anything" was a slap in the face. If we can land on the moon, they argued, then why cannot we fix poverty, racism, and end the war in Vietnam? To them, the moon landing was a symbol of a nation's misplaced priorities.

Project Apollo can also be remembered as the beginning to another story. Going to the moon was the inspiration behind the creation of the U.S. space program, and Apollo technology led directly to further

Too Hard to Fake It

The moon landings are among some of the most documented events in human history. Nevertheless, many people stubbornly believe that the Apollo Project was a hoax cooked up by the government and Hollywood film producers. When confronted with the hoax theory, Armstrong made this witty rebuttal: "I think that one would find that to perpetrate such a hoax accurately and without a few leaks around [NASA] would be much more difficult than actually going to the moon."[1]

space projects. Though the last Apollo mission splashed down in 1972, a *Saturn V* rocket, originally built for *Apollo 20*, launched the first U.S. space station. *Saturn V*'s third stage became *Skylab 1*, which hurtled into Earth orbit in May 1973. Thanks to Apollo spacecraft, astronauts were on their way to living months at a time in space, performing extensive experiments that could lay the groundwork for a lengthy trip to Mars.

Then, in July 1975, an Apollo command module flew one last historic mission, this time in Earth orbit. Project Apollo's final hour was a powerful

Moon Formation

Billions of years ago, a Mars-sized planet crashed into Earth, and the impact sent material flying into space. Then the swirling mass became the glowing disk in Earth's night sky. What happened after that?

At first, the force of the impact gave the moon a hot core, like Earth's. The hot core surrounded the moon in a magnetic field, which protected the moon's atmosphere from being stripped away by solar particles. But as the moon cooled, and its magnetic field ebbed, the atmosphere was soon lost.

Then, from 4.3 billion to 3.8 billion years ago, giant meteorites shot through space. They crashed into the surface of the moon and Earth. Because Earth's surface is constantly changing due to erosion and volcanic activity, evidence of those meteorites are long gone. On the moon, however, breccia rocks are a reminder of this long-lost era. Breccia formed as pulverized rock was fused together by the heat of the impact of meteorites.

The meteorites left wide craters on the moon's surface. Then, from 3.8 billion to 3.2 billion years ago, those craters filled with dark lava seeping up from the moon's core. The lava cooled, and large flat plains became the dark areas, or "seas," visible on the moon's face from Earth.

gesture of peace between the United States and the Soviet Union. The command module docked with a Soviet Soyuz spacecraft. The two crews greeted each other in space, and Deke Slayton, one of the original Mercury Seven astronauts, shook hands with cosmonaut Alexei Leonov, the world's first space walker. Such friendly overtures would have seemed a distant dream when Sputnik first sent its beeping radio signal from outer space.

For many, the scientific discoveries revealed by the moon landings make up the most exciting story. Apollo astronauts performed more than 50 experiments at six lunar sites. They brought back 842 pounds (382 kg) of lunar rock and soil samples, which were then examined by more than 1,000 scientists.

Samples revealed that moon rocks store bountiful deposits of precious metals and minerals, such as aluminum and iron. Could the minerals be mined one day for use on Earth? Could they one day be used as materials for a moon station? Even more remarkably,

Moon Junk

In addition to 60 scientific experiments, the Apollo astronauts left more than 90 tons of used equipment and other items on the lunar surface, including:

- Six landing stages.
- Three lunar rovers.
- 12 portable life support system backpacks.
- 12 pairs of lunar boots.
- Six American flags.
- Two golf balls.

moon rocks were shown to contain oxygen isotopes, like rocks on Earth. Could that oxygen be extracted to support life on the moon?

The answers to such questions are still unknown. After Project Apollo, NASA waited 22 years to return to the moon, this time with unmanned lunar probes. Then in 1998, further probes found important new evidence. There was ice in the moon's polar region.

Will astronauts walk on the moon again? At NASA, hopes are high. The space agency is working to send more astronauts to the moon by 2020. A station on the moon may be established, where astronauts could live and work for months at a time. The moon could serve as spectacular site for telescopic observations of the far reaches of the universe. It could also provide a base for further missions to Mars.

This much is clear. The story of the moon landing is far from over. How will Armstrong's "small step" be remembered in 100, 200, or 1,000 years? As with Christopher Columbus's landing in North America, the legacy of moon exploration could take centuries to reveal itself. Someday, those first footprints could be overshadowed, remembered as just the first wondrous step in a long journey of moon discovery.

Earth rising above the lunar horizon

TIMELINE

1957	1958	1959
On October 4, Soviets launch *Sputnik 1* into Earth orbit, and the space race begins.	In July, an act of Congress creates the U.S. National Aeronautics and Space Administration (NASA).	Soviet probe *Luna 2* becomes the first spacecraft to go to the moon on September 13.

1962	1965	1965
Aboard *Mercury 6*, John Glenn becomes the first American to orbit Earth on February 20.	Soviet cosmonaut Alexei Leonov becomes first human to exit a spacecraft and perform a space walk on March 18.	During the *Gemini 4* mission, Ed White becomes the first American to perform a space walk on June 3.

1961

Soviet cosmonaut Yuri Gagarin becomes the first human in space on April 12.

1961

Alan Shepherd becomes the first American to go into space on May 5.

1961

On May 25, President John F. Kennedy urges the nation to land a man on the moon "before the decade is out."

1965

Gemini 6 and *Gemini 7* perform the first space rendezvous on December 15.

1966

Gemini 8, commanded by Neil Armstrong, docks with an unmanned spacecraft on March 16.

1967

Apollo 1 astronauts die in a fire during preflight tests of the command module on January 27.

TIMELINE

1968	1968	1969
Apollo 7 orbits Earth from October 11–22, becoming the first manned flight of the Apollo Project.	*Apollo 8* becomes the first manned flight to orbit the moon on December 24.	*Apollo 9* tests out the complete Apollo spacecraft in Earth orbit, March 3–13.

1969	1969	1970
Apollo 11 splashes down in the Pacific Ocean on July 24.	*Apollo 12* astronauts touch down on the moon near *Surveyor 3* probe on November 19.	During April 11–17, *Apollo 13* mission nearly ends in disaster when an oxygen tank explodes.

1969

From May 18–26, *Apollo 10* tests out the lunar module in lunar orbit but does not land.

1969

Apollo 11 launches on July 16.

1969

On July 20, Neil Armstrong and Buzz Aldrin walk on the moon.

1971

Apollo 15 crew uses the first-ever lunar rover to travel on the moon on July 30.

1972

On April 20, *Apollo 16* touches down on the moon and uses the second lunar rover.

1972

Apollo 17 becomes the sixth and last Apollo mission to land on the moon on December 11.

ESSENTIAL FACTS

DATE OF EVENT
July 20, 1969

PLACE OF EVENT
The moon and Earth

KEY PLAYERS

❖ Neil Armstrong (astronaut)
❖ Buzz Aldrin (astronaut)
❖ Michael Collins (astronaut)
❖ John F. Kennedy (U.S. president 1961–1963)
❖ Richard Nixon (U.S. president 1969–1974)
❖ Mission Control

HIGHLIGHTS OF EVENT

❖ Congress created NASA in July 1958.

❖ President John F. Kennedy addressed Congress with his goal to land on the moon by the end of the decade.

❖ Apollo program began in January 1967. NASA scientists learn about the moon and prepare for the moon landing.

❖ Neil Armstrong and Buzz Aldrin became the first men to walk on the moon. The United States beat the Soviets to the moon.

❖ *Apollo 17* was the last Apollo mission to land on the moon.

❖ *Saturn 5* launched the space station *Skylab 1* in May 1973.

❖ Project Apollo ended on July 15, 1975. U.S. and Soviet astronauts met for the first time in space.

QUOTES

"We shall send to the moon, more than 240,000 miles from the control center in Houston, a giant rocket more than 300 feet tall, made of new metal alloys, some of which have not yet been invented, capable of standing heat and stresses several times more than have ever been experienced, fitted together with precision better than the finest watch, carrying all the equipment needed for propulsions, guidance, control, communications, food, and survival, on an untried mission to an unknown celestial body."

—John F. Kennedy

"That's one small step for a man, one giant leap for mankind."

—Neil Armstrong

ADDITIONAL RESOURCES

SELECT BIBLIOGRAPHY

Apollo. National Aeronautics and Space Administration. 6 Dec. 2006 <http://www.nasa.gov/mission_pages/apollo/index.html>.

Armstrong, Neil, Michael Collins, and Edwin E. Aldrin, Jr, with Gene Farmer and Dora Jane Hamblin. *First on the Moon*. Boston: Little, Brown and Company, 1970.

Cortright, Edgar M., ed. *Apollo Expeditions to the Moon*. Washington, D.C.: National Aeronautics and Space Administration, 1975.

Hurt, Harry III. *For All Mankind*. New York: Atlantic Monthly Press, 1988.

Reynolds, David West. *Apollo: The Epic Journey to the Moon*. San Diego: Tehabi Books, 2002.

Swanson, Glen E., ed. *"Before This Decade Is Out …" Personal Reflections on the Apollo Program*. Washington, D.C.: National Aeronautics and Space Administration, 1999.

To the Moon. Lone Wolf Pictures. Videocassette. Nova, 1999.

FURTHER READING

Dyson, Marianne J. *Home on the Moon: Living on a Space Frontier*. Washington, D.C.: National Geographic, 2003.

Spangenburg, Ray and Kit Moser. *The History of NASA*. New York: Franklin Watts, 2000.

Spangenburg, Ray and Kit Moser. *Project Apollo*. New York: Franklin Watts, 2001.

Thimmesh, Catherine. *Team Moon: How 400,000 People Landed Apollo 11 on the Moon*. Boston: Houghton Mifflin, 2006.

Web Links

To learn more about the Moon Landing, visit ABDO Publishing Company on the World Wide Web at **www.abdopublishing.com**. Web sites about Moon Landing are featured on our Book Links page. These links are routinely monitored and updated to provide the most current information available.

Places to Visit

Kennedy Space Center
Visitor Complex, Kennedy Space Center, FL 32899
321-449-4444
www.ksctickets.com
Learn about the history of NASA, see moon rocks, and possibly witness a Space Shuttle or rocket launch.

Smithsonian National Air and Space Museum
6th & Independence Ave., SW, Washington, DC 20560
202-633-1000
www.nasm.si.edu/museum/flagship.cfm
View the world's largest collection of historic spacecraft, including the *Apollo 11* command module.

Space Center Houston
1601 NASA Parkway, Houston, TX 77058
281-244-2100
www.spacecenter.org
Tour Mission Control, see Apollo spacecraft, and maybe even see real astronauts training for an upcoming mission.

GLOSSARY

communism
> A political philosophy in which all property is fairly shared by all citizens; in practice, communism has led to the governmental control of almost every aspect of people's lives.

cosmonaut
> A Russian (formerly Soviet) astronaut.

crater
> A large, bowl-shaped hollow in the ground, usually caused by the impact of a meteorite.

dock
> To join together in space.

feat
> An amazing accomplishment.

freeze dried
> Preserved by quickly freezing and then placing in a vacuum so that the ice turns to gas.

friction
> The resistance of two objects or surfaces (including air) rubbing against each other; friction slows down moving objects.

hull
> The main body of a ship or spacecraft.

lunar
> Having to do with the moon.

maneuver
> An operation, such as a flying technique, requiring skill.

meteorite
> A chunk of stone or metal that flies through space and crashes into the moon or Earth.

microgravity
> The condition in outer space in which the pull of gravity is very weak.

micrometeoroid
> A particle of dust flying through space; micrometeoroids burn up in Earth's atmosphere but are an extreme hazard on the moon.

myth
> A story often repeated and passed down through generations; myths often explain the nature of the universe.

navigation
> The science of figuring out one's position and route, especially in places with few landmarks such as outer space and the oceans.

orbit
> The curved path a spacecraft flies around a moon or planet; to follow such a path.

probe
> An unmanned spacecraft used for exploring new places and sending back information to Earth.

quarantine
> To keep a person away from other people for a period of time in order to prevent the spread of disease.

rendezvous
> To meet up, but not physically join together, in space.

satellite
> A piece of equipment sent in orbit around a planet or the moon in order to gather or transmit information.

simulator
> Equipment that simulates, or copies, a real experience; before going into outer space, astronauts learn how to fly their spacecraft in flight simulators.

thrust
> The force that propels a rocket.

vacuum
> A completely empty space, void even of air.

weightlessness
> The condition in outer space during which astronauts float around the spacecraft as if they weighed nothing.

Source Notes

Chapter 1. Lift Off

1. John F. Kennedy. "Moon Speech—Rice Stadium, September 12, 1962." Johnson Space Center. 8 Dec. 2006 <http://www1.jsc.nasa.gov/er/seh/ricetalk.htm>.
2. Harry Hurt III. *For All Mankind.* New York: The Atlantic Monthly Press, 1988. 48.
3. Edgar M. Cortright, ed. *Apollo Expeditions to the Moon.* Washington, D.C.: National Aeronautics and Space Administration, 1975. 203.

Chapter 2. The Race to the Moon

1. *To the Moon.* Lone Wolf Pictures. Videocassette. Nova, 1999.
2. David West Reynolds. *Apollo: The Epic Journey to the Moon.* San Diego: Tehabi Books, 2002. 41.
3. John F. Kennedy. "Memorandum for Vice President, 20 April 1961." NASA. 8 Dec. 2006 <http://history.nasa.gov/Apollomon/apollo1.pdf>.
4. Harry Hurt III. *For All Mankind.* New York: The Atlantic Monthly Press, 1988. 52.
5. John F. Kennedy. "Moon Speech—Rice Stadium, September 12, 1962." Johnson Space Center. 8 Dec. 2006 <http://www1.jsc.nasa.gov/er/seh/ricetalk.htm>.
6. John F. Kennedy. "Special Message to the Congress on Urgent National Needs." John F. Kennedy Presidential Library & Museum. 25 May 1961. 8 Dec. 2006 <http://www.jfklibrary.org/Historical+Resources/Archives/Reference+Desk/Speeches/JFK/003POF03NationalNeeds05251961.htm>.

Chapter 3. Preparations

1. Edgar M. Cortright, ed. *Apollo Expeditions to the Moon.* Washington, D.C.: National Aeronautics and Space Administration, 1975. ix.
2. Harry Hurt III. *For All Mankind.* New York: The Atlantic Monthly Press, 1988. 154.
3. Buzz Aldrin and Malcolm McConnell. *Men from Earth.* New York: Bantam Books, 1989. 91.
4. Neil Armstrong, Michael Collins, and Edwin E. Aldrin, Jr. *First on the Moon.* Boston: Little, Brown and Company, 1970. 40.
5. *To the Moon.* Lone Wolf Pictures. Videocassette. Nova, 1999.

Chapter 4. Trial Runs

1. "Why Explore the Universe?" timeforkids.com. 6 Dec. 2006 <http://www.timeforkids.com/TFK/media/teachers/pdfs/2003S/0302 14WRI.pdf>.
2. Kelly A. Giblin. "'Fire in the Cockpit!' Apollo 1 Was the Greatest Disaster in America's Race to the Moon." AmericanHeritage.com 13.4 (Spring 1988). 6 Dec. 2006 <www.americanheritage.com/articles/ magazine/it/1998/4/1998_4_46.shtml>.
3. Ibid.
4. *To the Moon.* Lone Wolf Pictures. Videocassette. Nova, 1999.
5. Ibid.
6. Michael Light and Andrew Chaikin. *Full Moon.* New York: Alfred A. Knopf, 1999. 7.
7. David West Reynolds. *Apollo: The Epic Journey to the Moon.* San Diego: Tehabi Books, 2002. 108.
8. *To the Moon.* Lone Wolf Pictures. Videocassette. Nova, 1999.

Chaper 5. Journey Through Space

1. Harry Hurt III. *For All Mankind.* New York: The Atlantic Monthly Press, 1988. 60.
2. Ibid. 66.
3. Ibid. 65.

Chapter 6. Moon Landing

1. Harry Hurt III. *For All Mankind.* New York: The Atlantic Monthly Press, 1988. 126.
2. "Apollo 11, the First Landing." BBC. 1 Sept. 2000. 6 Dec. 2006 <http://www.bbc.co.uk/dna/h2g2/A429086>.
3. Edgar M. Cortright, ed. *Apollo Expeditions to the Moon.* Washington, D.C.: National Aeronautics and Space Administration, 1975. 207.
4. "Why Explore the Universe?" timeforkids.com. 6 Dec. 2006 <http://www.timeforkids.com/TFK/media/teachers/pdfs/2003S/0302 14WRI.pdf>.
5. Neil Armstrong, Michael Collins, and Edwin E. Aldrin, Jr. First on the Moon. Boston: Little, Brown and Company, 1970. 276.
6. Ibid. 278.

Source Notes Continued

7. Harry Hurt III. *For All Mankind.* New York: The Atlantic Monthly Press, 1988. 143.

8. Harry Hurt III. *For All Mankind.* New York: The Atlantic Monthly Press, 1988. 162.

9. Ibid. 165.

10. David West Reynolds. *Apollo: The Epic Journey to the Moon.* San Diego: Tehabi Books, 2002. 136.

11. Ibid. 136.

12. *To the Moon.* Lone Wolf Pictures. Videocassette. Nova, 1999.

13. Ibid. 167.

Chapter 7. One Giant Leap

1. Neil Armstrong, Michael Collins, and Edwin E. Aldrin, Jr. *First on the Moon.* Boston: Little, Brown and Company, 1970. 320.

2. James R. Hansen. "Armstrong, Neil Alden." World Book Online Reference Center. 2006. 9 Dec. 2006 <http://www.worldbookonline.com/wb/Article?id=ar031060>.

3. Neil Armstrong, Michael Collins, and Edwin E. Aldrin, Jr. *First on the Moon.* Boston: Little, Brown and Company, 1970. 323.

4. National Aeronautics and Space Administration, Office of Public Affairs. *The First Lunar Landing As Told by the Astronauts: 20th Anniversary.* Washington, D.C.: National Aeronautics and Space Administration: 1989. 11.

5. Harry Hurt III. *For All Mankind.* New York: The Atlantic Monthly Press, 1988. 185.

6. Neil Armstrong, Michael Collins, and Edwin E. Aldrin, Jr. *First on the Moon.* Boston: Little, Brown and Company, 1970. 332–333.

Chapter 8. Back to Earth

1. Neil Armstrong, Michael Collins, and Edwin E. Aldrin, Jr. *First on the Moon.* Boston: Little, Brown and Company, 1970. 361.

2. Harry Hurt III. *For All Mankind.* New York: The Atlantic Monthly Press, 1988. 255–256.

3. *To the Moon.* Lone Wolf Pictures. Videocassette. Nova, 1999.

4. Harry Hurt III. *For All Mankind.* New York: The Atlantic Monthly Press, 1988. 285.

5. Ibid. 291.

6. Neil Armstrong, Michael Collins, and Edwin E. Aldrin, Jr. *First on the Moon.* Boston: Little, Brown and Company, 1970. 403.
7. Richard Nixon. "Remarks to Apollo Astronauts Aboard the U.S.S. Hornet Following Completion of Their Lunar Mission." *The American Presidency Project.* 24 July 1969. 9 Dec. 2006 <http://www.presidency. ucsb.edu/ws/print.php?pid=2138>.
8. Ibid. 409.

Chapter 9. Later Missions

1. David West Reynolds. Apollo: *The Epic Journey to the Moon.* San Diego: Tehabi Books, 2002. 148.
2. Andrew Chaikin. "Thirty Years Ago: Apollo 14's Explorations Continue." Space.com. 6 Feb. 2001. 6 Dec. 2006 <http://www.space. com/news/spacehistory/a14_continues_010206.html>.
3. "Apollo Missions: The Conclusion." BBC. 17 Sept. 2000. 6 Dec. 2006 <http://www.bbc.co.uk/dna/h2g2/A830774>.

Chapter 10. Moon Legacy

1. Harry Hurt III. *For All Mankind.* New York: The Atlantic Monthly Press, 1988. 324.

INDEX

ABOUT THE AUTHOR

Nadia Higgins has been a children's book editor and writer since 2001. Before that, she worked as a magazine editor and journalist. She especially enjoys writing about science and nature. Ms. Higgins lives in Minneapolis, Minnesota, with her husband and two daughters.

PHOTO CREDITS